CODEPENDENT NO MORE

PRACTICAL GUIDANCE TO FIX YOUR CODEPENDENCY, STOP BEING A PEOPLE PLEASER, AND START LOVING YOURSELF

ANDREI NEDELCU

Copyright © 2020 by Andrei Nedelcu - All rights reserved.

This document aims to provide exact and reliable information in regards to the topic and issue covered. The publication is sold with the idea that the publisher is not required to render accounting, officially permitted, or otherwise, qualified services. If advice is necessary, legal or professional, a practiced individual in the profession should be ordered.

- From a Declaration of Principles which was accepted and approved equally by a Committee of the American Bar Association and a Committee of Publishers and Associations.

No part of this document should be reproduced, duplicated, or transmitted by any means, either in electronic or printed format. Recording this publication is strictly prohibited and any storage of this document is not allowed unless with written permission from the publisher. All rights reserved.

The information provided herein is stated to be truthful and consistent, and any liability arising from inattention or otherwise, wrong usage or abuse of any policies, processes, or directions contained within is the solitary and utter responsibility of the recipient reader. Under no circumstances will any legal responsibility or blame be held against the publisher for any reparation, damages, or monetary loss due to the information herein, either directly or indirectly.

Respective authors own all copyrights not held by the publisher.

The information herein is offered for informational purposes only and is universal as so. The presentation of the information is without a contract or any type of guarantee assurance.

The trademarks that are used are without any consent, and the publication of the trademark is without permission or backing by the trademark owner. All trademarks and brands within this book are for clarifying purposes only and are owned by the owners themselves, not affiliated with this document.

CONTENTS

Introduction	7
Do you want healthy relationships?	9
1. Codependency: How do I recognize it?	11
2. What do codependent relationships look like?	19
3. I'm codependent, now what?	25
4. How to stop being a people-pleaser	33
5. I'm so confused, sad, and lonely. What can I do?	43
6. The best way to STOP your codependency	51
7. Start to gain autonomy	65
8. The Secret of Detachment	71
9. The courage to change: START to paint your goals	77
10. Smart simple principles to beat codependency	83
Conclusion	91
Do you feel incomplete without your partner?	93
Notes	95
Bibliography	99

DEAR READER,

I have news that will for sure delight you! I have created a superb and special list of affirmations meant to help with your fight against codependency. It is a pleasure and honor for me, which I cannot describe in words, to hand them over to you as a GIFT.

These affirmations, which are extremely valuable and tested throughout my practice, can be printed out and pasted in strategic and visible places. Places that you go by often! Personally, I like to see them as often as possible, at home but at work too.

I'm absolutely convinced that these treasures will be of great use to you and will help you fight with different elements and states/moods caused by codependency!

Thus, you can access this nicely designed Cheat-Sheet that will play a huge role in your recovery right away by just downloading it.

Stay safe! I have trust that you can climb higher than I can lead you myself!

SCAN THE QR CODE BELOW TO DOWNLOAD YOUR CHEAT-SHEET

INTRODUCTION

I am honored that you are interested in reading this book dedicated to people with codependency traits. Throughout this book, I have done my best to address the main issues related to codependency and offer practical and evidence-based solutions. In other words, this book is more practical than theoretical. It gets to the heart of the issue.

Although many books have been written on this topic, most treat the issues superficially or give you only limited information about how to tackle codependency. It is difficult and overwhelming to feel responsible for the entire world. Some people constantly give to others but have no idea of how to receive. Some people give until they have nothing left to give. When things get worse, they begin to doubt themselves and become depressed, anxious, fearful, and emotionally paralyzed. They feel trapped. Pain and insecurity start to manifest in all facets of their life. They lose their independence. They are afraid to make decisions. They are no longer satisfied with their life.

In this book, I focus on specific and clear issues and do my best to avoid unnecessary clichés. If you are wondering what codependency is and how to overcome it, this book is for you. Thank you for your attention and interest.

After reading this book, you will have a better chance of developing confidence, ending the pain, and gaining control of your life. **Until then, take care!**

DO YOU WANT HEALTHY RELATIONSHIPS?

Scan the QR code to discover what *not* to do when you find yourself free from a codependent relationship

- Dan

"A must-read to break free from codependency! I'm convinced that you'll learn so much more about yourself by reading this book than other popular codependency books because it is so practical and the exercises it has for each chapter really makes you reflect! It is easy to read, very straightforward, and to conclude, this book will hug your brain and heart (sic) with empowering messages and exercises that will assist your recovery process. Highly recommend!"

- Stela

"This book will help you set boundaries without ruining relationships and also make you see the bad habits you have because of codependency! The go-to resource for people dealing with codependency!"

CODEPENDENCY: HOW DO I RECOGNIZE IT?

"Freedom cannot be bestowed — it must be achieved."

— ELBERT HUBBARD

Many books have been written about codependency, each with its own definition of the term. Unfortunately, most of these books provide little or no insight into the causes of codependency and how to remedy them.

These books describe codependency in scary and painful terms. Many undesirable behavioral patterns are listed as codependency traits. The funny thing is that you will probably recognize many of these problems by the time you have finished reading those books but still will not be able to describe exactly what those issues are. Moreover, because you can't explain your problems, you are left without the tools to fight them, so you are back to square one.

Therefore, I have decided to describe the true nature of these problems as clearly as possible. By the end of the first two chapters, you should have a clear insight into the issues and the tools to accurately identify them.

LET'S GET STRAIGHT TO THE POINT: WHAT DOES CODEPENDENCY REALLY MEAN?

Initially, the term "codependent" was used to refer to a person in a relationship with a person struggling with a substance use disorder, for example, an alcoholic.[1] That is why most of these books only refer to those who find themselves in this particular situation. We can conclude that codependent people live in unhealthy relationships where emotions are ignored, constrained, or punished. If you live in an environment where there has been some form of emotional neglect or abuse, you may develop difficulties and problems that will significantly affect your relationships and how you feel.

Codependency is ultimately a loss of freedom.

In other words, codependency is a relationship in which you invest so much in another person that you can no longer function independently. Simply put, your mood, happiness, identity, trust, and values depend on that other person.

Codependency involves the loss of personal autonomy: all thoughts, emotions, behaviors, and decisions are defined by somebody else. You always need the other person's approval and validation to feel good.[2] An experienced psychotherapist once said that we can talk about codependency when there is almost always "the need to be needed." For example, it will be difficult for you to say no to an offer that does not interest you, and if you do, you will feel ashamed and guilty because you dared to do such a "bad thing." In the next chapter, I will explain codependency in greater detail and give more examples so you can better understand the problem and how to overcome it.

WHEN DOES CODEPENDENCY BECOME PATHOLOGICAL?

I intend to give the reader three important keys to determine if they suffer from codependency. Over time, I have given these diagnostic tools to the patients I have worked with:

1. Codependency is a problem when it significantly affects our behavior

Here we are talking about professional and personal behavior. It is time to notice the red warning light when you realize your behavior is being impacted. If you are missing out on good opportunities because of specific behavior patterns, it means there is an issue that needs to be addressed.

2. Codependency is a problem when it significantly affects our relationships

If we constantly allow our insecurities to show and our relationships to be affected by fluctuations in our mood, identity, decisions, and trust, those around us will want to distance themselves from us. In short, it will be difficult to maintain a real friendship or a romantic relationship.

3. Codependency becomes a problem when it affects our well-being

Codependency creates discomfort; we feel bad and have intense damaging negative emotions. We are fearful and doubting; we lack a sense of trust in ourselves and carry feelings of guilt, shame, and inadequacy. These feelings can manifest as somatic symptoms such as various aches and pains: physiological, emotional, cognitive, behavioral, etc.

WHAT CAUSES CODEPENDENCY?

You may be tired of hearing about the childhood influences that affect you and how you think. But data repeatedly confirms that problems develop at an early stage.[3] So it is natural to ask ourselves where our issues originate. From childhood, we begin to draw on different beliefs about the world and life; we go through different life experiences and develop coping skills.

One of the leading causes **is abuse or neglect**. Living in an abusive relationship or environment may lead us to conclude that we are unimportant and have no value. **Our environment does not affect us as much as the beliefs and lessons the mind has learned from living in that environment.**[4] Therefore, codependency traits develop specifically to fight these feelings of uselessness and inadequacy. For example, we may take on the role of caregiver towards an alcoholic in order to feel needed. Or we may try to cure someone's mental disorder or addiction to make ourselves feel good. Saving others can give us a fleeting sense of validation and importance; however, this harms us in the long run.

Varying parenting styles may be another cause of codependency. For example, you may have had an overprotective parent—this could increase the likelihood of developing codependency. On the other hand, maybe you had a great environment. So what caused the problem? It may be because you were not given the independence needed to grow. Some parents make all the decisions, so children learn to disregard their own beliefs and thoughts. Gradually, that child thinks, "What I feel is not important; other people's approval is more important."

In our minds, it doesn't matter if the experiences were positive or negative. What matters are the patterns and beliefs we have formed.[5] If our experiences have taught us that we are inadequate, irrelevant, and flawed, then codependency issues will develop.

So, the negative environment we grew up in and the people who harmed us directly or indirectly are not the enemy. Our real enemies are the beliefs and thoughts we have formed from those experiences. The bitter truth is that we cannot erase or change the past, but we can work on the beliefs imprinted in our minds. And that's why I decided to write this book, to help you change these flawed and damaging beliefs. In a later chapter, we will learn how to challenge the thinking that fuels codependency, so it loses the power it has over us.

PRACTICAL SECTION: LET'S DO IT!

Each chapter will include a practical section that will help you understand the problems we face. I will often use a rating scale from 1 to 10 (where one means nothing or almost nothing, and ten means a lot). Use a separate sheet of paper or a diary to answer these questions. Take your time. Take time to reflect on your answers and review everything you have achieved:

- Use your own words to define addiction in your case.
- How did codependency develop in your life?

- On a scale of 1 to 10, how much does this affect your results, relationships, and feelings?
- Write down three situations that happened this week in which you showed autonomy (the ability to solve things on your own).

2

WHAT DO CODEPENDENT RELATIONSHIPS LOOK LIKE?

"The acknowledgment of a single possibility can change everything."

— ABERJHANI

Codependency is not recognized as an official mental disorder. Therefore, this problem is not in the DSMV (Diagnostic and Statistical Manual of Mental Disorders, 5th Edition). However, a lot of the symptoms overlap with other personality disorders. Below, I will detail the main symptoms, but it is important to understand that you don't have to have all these traits be identified as having a codependency issue.[1] You may have only one, or you may have many. But they will affect your quality of life.

1. LOW SELF-ESTEEM

Codependency can strongly affect our self-image. We perceive ourselves as weak, worthless, stupid, and unattractive if we are unable to help those around us. As a result, we feel ashamed and useless, so we look to other people to determine our value.

2. THE NEED TO SAVE OTHERS

Don't get me wrong—being kind and empathetic to those around us is fine, but this trait can lead us to believe that we must protect our loved ones from all the evil in the world. Therefore, if someone close to you does something wrong, you want to "fix" the situation. And this can become destructive for them and you because it prevents them from becoming independent, taking responsibility, and thus learning from their own mistakes. If someone close to you is addicted, you work very hard caring for them, enabling their addiction, and stopping them from recovering in a healthy manner.

3. CONTINUOUS DENIAL (SELF-DENIAL)

A codependent person will almost always put others first and prioritize their happiness and well-being over their own. Simply put, this person will deny that they need rest, emotional support, care, empathy, and love. If they conclude that they need all this, the first tendency will be to feel guilt, shame, or anxiety. As their focus is always on others, this person tends to be anxious if someone offers help.

4. THE NEED TO BE A PEOPLE-PLEASER

If you find yourself in a situation where you almost always change your plans, thoughts, behavior, and emotions "so everyone can benefit," you are a people-pleaser. You crave validation. You need to be appreciated, wanted, or loved. If someone is unhappy, you begin to feel anxious. For example, if someone suggests going out, and you don't feel up to it, you will not say how you feel – you will still go out. In romantic relationships, you always try to be perfect and do things perfectly. You feel bad refusing anything offered to you or talking about how you feel. The often-used word of a person who always wants to please others is YES.

5. DYSFUNCTIONAL BOUNDARIES

If your self-esteem is affected, it will be reflected in the behavior and the limits you impose, whether it concerns material, physical, emotional, or mental limitations. Usually, people who have suffered from various forms of childhood abuse have difficulty setting proper boundaries. Limits can be affected in many areas of life, for example, when it is crucial to say, "No, thank you; that bothers me."

6. LOW EMOTIONAL EXPRESSIVITY

Because you always believe that what you think, feel or imagine doesn't matter much, it may be quite difficult to identify how you really feel in different situations. This is because you taught your mind to believe that "It doesn't really matter what I feel anyway," "It's not so relevant anyway," "Nobody cares anyway." There may also be difficulties in communicating honestly, with communication being static, routine, and superficial.

7. TOO MUCH ADDICTION AND FEAR OF REJECTION

You have become used to putting aside your own interests over the years and, consequently, neglect yourself completely. Your life revolves around others, and you have no interest in your own hobbies, emotions, goals, or needs. What other people decide for you is much more important than what you decide for yourself. Their decisions are more important than yours. Do you find it difficult to initiate personal projects, implement your ideas, or have personal ideas?

Being so connected to the person you love, you may fear being alone or rejected. This is because they are empowered to satisfy the needs you have. Therefore, you may fear rejection or abandonment or interpret neutral indicators as clear signals of rejection.

Other symptoms include feeling responsible for other people's emotions, decisions, thoughts, and well-being; anticipating other people's needs; trying to please others instead of looking after your needs; being attracted to people who have different needs; being bored and feeling empty and worthless if those around you do not have a major crisis in their life or a problem to solve; often feeling angry, victimized, unappreciated and used.

People with codependency problems often come from dysfunctional or problematic families (although not always). They deny their family has issues or shortcomings, blame themselves for absolutely everything, reject compliments or praises, are convinced that they are not good enough, feel ashamed of what they are, settle for being needed, push their thoughts and feelings as far away as possible because of fear and guilt, and have significant communication difficulties.

Right off the bat, I want to clarify that I have only drawn a few guidelines for you to follow. You may struggle with other symptoms not described in this book. Every mind is different, so the symptoms and experiences can differ. I chose to focus more on the treatment side because many resources and texts describe the problems that might arise in more depth, in too much depth, perhaps. Instead, I want to leave you with an accurate tool to identify the symptoms and put things together.[2] Here is the link that can be accessed.

PRACTICAL SECTION: LET'S DO OUR BEST!

- Add to the list of the symptoms above. Build your list of symptoms. Try to go through other materials as well if this list is insufficient.
- For each symptom, use a number rating scale from 1-10 with a corresponding symptom (e.g., self-denial: 9, people pleaser: 4).
- Which symptoms have the highest scores and produce the most distress?

3

I'M CODEPENDENT, NOW WHAT?

"Don't you know that nobody can make you be shit? You can only let it happen."

— JUXIAN TANG, ZERO TOLERANCE

As mentioned in previous chapters, we will begin slowly and then give more attention to the things that cause pain and distress. But for this, we must establish a few basic things right from the start.

You are special.

Being codependent, we become used to living in the shadow of our loved ones and eventually conclude that we are not as important. When we value the approval of others more than we value ourselves, we invalidate our own needs.

Therefore, this chapter is dedicated to those who "don't need anything from anyone." I write these words for those who minimize their own failures, whose repressed and unfulfilled desires and plans don't matter. These lines are for those whose thoughts are unimportant and whose problems are not worth mentioning. These lines are for those who constantly repeat: "I don't deserve anything; it doesn't matter anyway; it wasn't that relevant anyway; I don't need anything special."

I write for those convinced that having needs and expressing them is unimportant, so they stopped having them. Or whose own thoughts are blunted and buried. These lines are for those who have learned that denial and self-invalidation is the most effective way to protect themselves from disappointment. They believe their needs are unimportant and will not be met. Since those close to us tend to deny our needs, it seems normal for us to deny them too. Because we are trying to avoid pain, denial and self-invalidation can become the main strategy to deal with things.

I could never fully comprehend why others are more important than us. Why wouldn't our needs matter as much? Why shouldn't we be as special as them? It doesn't matter if you are wanted or not; you are just as special and important as everybody else. Denial is one of the main symptoms of codependency. It is a defense mechanism that works subconsciously and without you realizing it.[1] To protect yourself from being hurt, you use a mechanism called self-denial.

Simply put, you start to deny your own emotions and thoughts. You lose touch with your own feelings. You refuse to express yourself and say what bothers you. You might even deny that you have codependency traits. You look at things and your situation as if you had no choice. You do everything possible to avoid pain. You put aside your own needs and feel ashamed that you think about them. You compromise your own values and integrity to avoid rejection. This protects you in the short term but will harm you in the long run. In some specific situations, denial is not necessarily wrong, but it does not solve things in the long term.

Maybe you ended up fighting and struggling with anxiety, depression, worries, a high level of stress, and a sense of your own value. If you have reached this point because of a situation that has pushed you into codependency, now is the time to be honest and see the problem as it is. In my book, *How Does Cognitive Behavioral Therapy Work*, I discussed these issues in-depth. If you believe you are suffering from any of these issues, I think it might be good for you to read through it.

Next, I want to give you some cognitive-behavioral strategies to help you stop this pattern of denial and start doing things in a much healthier manner. I want to warn you that it will not be easy. Nevertheless, I am confident you can progressively apply the tools I offer.

1. GRADUALLY START TALKING ABOUT YOUR OWN NEEDS

This is precisely what it says. Allow yourself to think about something you need, for example, attention. Try talking to someone else about this. If it is too difficult, start writing in your journal about your needs or emotions. Start telling your loved ones how you feel. If you want a better chance of success, plan things well: tonight at 9 p.m., when my husband finishes eating, I will tell him that I feel tired, exhausted, and sad. If this is difficult for you, I will try to offer you additional winning strategies in a later chapter.

This is as important for you as it is for others. Their feelings are not more important than yours. Their unhappiness is not more important than yours. Many of our needs are also legitimate. Those needs can be fulfilled. Even though talking about such things may initially make us apprehensive, do not shy away from your pain and emotions. Don't be afraid to release these feelings. This is the opposite of denial; this means acceptance. Accept that you feel bad. Accept that some behaviors are NOT okay, and they negatively affect you. Accept and try to talk about how your feel.

2. LEARN TO RECOGNIZE WHEN YOUR NEEDS ARE A SIGN OF WEAKNESS

Acknowledge that we have specific emotional or physical needs that make us vulnerable. Create an observation grid and note each time you feel powerless. Over time, by doing this, this feeling will diminish. Even if feeling vulnerable seems strange, dangerous, and something to be scared of, you will be safe if you show your vulnerability to the right people. So make a list of every situation where you see needs as a weakness. This list will be beneficial to you later in the battle with codependency.

3. STOP APOLOGIZING FOR YOUR OWN NEEDS

When you dare to speak up and say what you think and feel, you are not violating any code of conduct. You are doing what an independent person does. The tendency is to feel guilty and sorry that you dared to have your own thoughts. But it is acceptable to want something, have needs, and have your own ideas. You are also within your rights to ask for something. You are not doing anything wrong by doing so, so stop apologizing. Instead, thank the person who listens to you when you say, "I need you to listen to me for a few minutes. I don't feel very well. Thank you for taking the time to listen to me."

When you apologize for what you need, you subtly convey to your mind that it's problematic to want what you want.

Therefore, stop APOLOGIZING. Start saying, Thank you. "I want or need that thing, and thank you."

4. DON'T LOWER YOUR EXPECTATIONS

Because we have become accustomed to neglecting ourselves, we have learned to anticipate the fact that others "will not value us." So you minimize the importance of your own feelings and needs. And so, you run scenarios about how busy others are, how what they do is so important, and how your problems, on the other hand, are not serious. If others insist and pay attention to your concerns, you feel afraid. You are not used to such treatment. You consider them transient. Surely, you will be disappointed afterward, right? So why even bother?

As mentioned above, try to have the same standards for yourself as you have for those around you. If they deserve a lot, you certainly deserve a lot. It's okay to have expectations. You are just as important as them. Don't ever forget it!

Imagine your recovery as a step ladder.

The first step is precisely the one we discussed in this chapter. Start by eliminating all traces of denial. You will need patience and awareness, which are essential for this process. This is a complicated process, but the effort will be worth it. This chapter will probably not be enough to win the battle against denial, but it is undoubtedly a good starting point. In the following chapters, I will try to help you apply various tools to increase your chances of success. Also, please use the practical section at the end of the chapter to assist you. And now, let's move on to the next step. Walk with me with confidence!

PRACTICAL SECTION: LET'S DO IT!

- On a scale of 1-10, how much do you avoid discussing your needs?
- In which context would you try to talk about your needs, and what will you say?
- Which situations are you most in denial about?
- Write down three reasons why your needs are as important as those of the people around you.
- How many times this week did you apologize for your own needs?
- Choose three situations in which you will make a request followed by a "thank you," not an apology. Write with specifics: place, time, and what you will say (more or less).
- On a scale of 1-10, how important is what I think, feel, or receive?

JUST A QUICK REMINDER...

To help you win the fight against codependency, I've created a Cheat-Sheet (ten valuable affirmations) that you can print out and stick on your fridge or any other visible place.

Before turning the page, make sure you download your **free Cheat-Sheet** by scanning the QR code below:

4

HOW TO STOP BEING A PEOPLE-PLEASER

"I speak to everyone in the same way, whether he is the garbage man or the president of the University."

— ALBERT EINSTEIN

Being a people-pleaser means that you almost always say YES, even though you know very well that the right answer is NO. No, you don't want to buy that product. No, you don't want to take advantage of that glorious offer either. No, you don't even want to go out with your girlfriend tonight because you don't feel great. No, you don't want to. But still, you say YES, and that's how things start going downhill. And if you experience codependency traits, there is a high probability that these symptoms will often upset and overwhelm you.

The fact that you want to make others happy is noteworthy. It is a wonderful thing, and I salute you for it. Showing kindness and generosity to those around you is admirable. We show true camaraderie when we put the needs of others above our desires.

However, many of us tend to exaggerate these wonderful traits. We reach the point where we strive to make others happy at the expense of our own needs. And that's when that kindness and generosity become a problem.

First of all, we can't make someone happy. Of course, we can bring them joy and brighten their day, but we cannot control each person's level of happiness directly.[1]

WHAT HAPPENS WHEN WE ARE PEOPLE-PLEASERS?

Usually, when we try to please those around us, we use a form of communication that is not particularly helpful in relationships. It's called passive communication. In other words, what we do is stay silent about what we feel or the needs we have. We bury our heads in the ground and say YES to everything when our heart and mind are saying ABSOLUTELY NO. I don't want to go out with you. The data from specialized literature are quite clear in this regard. This type of communication tends to create a lot of problems. Whether we like it or not, we all have different needs. When we repress them over a long time, it can lead to resentment and then to passive-aggressive communication or communication based on aggression.[2]

At the same time, passive communication can be quite awkward for the other person because it sends contradictory messages. If we say yes, while our non-verbal language is saying no, it is quite frustrating for those around us. Therefore, long term, passive communication can lead to anxiety, depression, stress, burnout, or low self-esteem.[3] Basically, what we convey to the mind when we use passive communication is this: "The needs of others are important, but mine are not." Progressively, we devalue ourselves.

WHAT DOES AGGRESSIVE COMMUNICATION MEAN?

Most people use one of these three types of communication: passive, aggressive, or assertive. They may also use a combination of all three. People who use an aggressive communication style usually take what is theirs no matter what. They are often considered bullies and do not take into account the needs, feelings, and opinions of others. They may claim some form of self-justification or appear superior. They often humiliate and intimidate those around them or may even ultimately threaten them.[4]

The main reason is that this is how they learned to get what they want. So, finally, things are making sense, aren't they?

Still, how can you stop being a people-pleaser?

The best type of communication is **assertive communication**.[5] Over time, I have worked hard to help patients develop this skill. It is a skill that can be learned, and I want to help you develop it. First, I wish to point out that this type of communication is based on mutual respect. It is effective and diplomatic. Being assertive means you respect yourself, are willing to fight for your interests, and can openly express this.

Assertive communication gives you the best chance of successfully delivering your message. This form of communication is direct and respectful. If you are used to communicating in a more passive manner, you may feel that this type of communication initially seems quite aggressive.

When we say **assertive communication,** we mean that you can express your ideas and feelings positively and negatively —everything in the most open, honest, and direct way possible.

The main benefits include expressing your needs, desires, ideas, and feelings. You will notice that as you get better at it, you will gain more confidence, and your self-esteem will increase. Also, you will start to recognize your emotions better; this will come automatically. At the same time, from my experience with patients, I noticed that most of them end up earning other people's respect simply because they are able to verbalize what they need. And so the situation will improve for you and those around you. You will gradually notice your anxiety decreasing, and the stress associated with repressing your needs will reduce considerably.

There are a few key things to keep in mind:

1. Evaluate your style of communication

We tend to use a specific communication style, depending on our experience. But, of course, everything happens subconsciously and without our realizing it.

So, do you tend to express your thoughts or keep quiet? When you finish all your tasks, do you usually AGREE to take on additional ones? Before making changes, be aware of how you communicate. Is your communication style passive, aggressive, or assertive? Be guided by the descriptions I have given you. If you are unsure, ask someone who knows you to tell you which one best describes you.

2. Simple but very relevant indicators:

- **Eye contact:** demonstrates interest in the conversation and conveys sincerity; therefore, look at the person you are talking to. Don't look out the window when you want to be heard. If you find it difficult to look into a person's eyes—start practicing. As often as you can, deliberately look at someone straight in the eye, and gradually, you will overcome your inability to maintain eye contact. If it is too difficult, choose a photo of a beautiful person and stare into their eyes. Over time, it will become easier and more fun. But beware! Don't overdo this strategy. In time you will know how long it is comfortable for the other person to be stared at.

- **Body posture:** stand up straight in front of the other person, and keep your hands out of your pocket, please. Keep your back straight, your chest forward.
- **Gestures**: help to build relationships and show the control you have. Be aware of them.
- **Voice**: a crucial aspect is the timbre and tone (according to the situation). Some situations require a slight raise of the voice, others a significant lowering. But I trust that you will also become an expert in this regard.
- **Timing**: make sure to judge the best moment and place when you want to say something. For example, if you want to say something sensitive to your partner, look around; if he is celebrating with friends, you will probably conclude that this is not the right time. One of the most valuable lessons I have learned from patients is that the same thing said at different times can bring about very different results. So, make sure the timing is in your favor.
- **Content**: the way you convey your thoughts, emotions, opinions, upsets, etc., is much more

important than what you actually have to say. Therefore, let's practice.

STRATEGY. HOW EXACTLY DO WE PROCEED?

1. Be direct and use the personal pronoun "I."

When I say it is crucial to be direct, I mean it is essential to focus on three major elements: behavior, emotions, and consequences. Let me use an example:

"I feel sad when you are late for meetings. I think it's disrespectful."

"I feel unappreciated when you don't listen to me. I don't like talking to myself."

"You hurt me so much when you told me that. I don't like you using those words."

2. Behavior Rehearsal

It is a strategy that involves practicing appropriate behavior responses within specific situations. It won't feel natural initially, but eventually, it will not be necessary to practice. Don't forget the other person, the targeted behavior, emotions, and how they all relate to you. You will probably realize, with practice, that you will no longer be so afraid to do this in real life. You can practice with your friends too; it will be fun. You don't necessarily have to share only negative things. For example: "I feel appreciated when you listen to me. I realize I'm important to you." Practice until it comes as naturally as possible for you to do it.

3. The broken record

I suggest you use this approach with badly-behaved and manipulative people, for example, (no offense) those who want to sell you unwanted insurance. This technique will build your confidence because it encourages you to ignore all the verbal traps meant to influence you. If you learn to use it well, you can neutralize irrelevant arguments as you state your point of view. Simply put, this technique involves calmly reiterating your decision and letting go of whatever is holding you back. You will find that you don't necessarily need to scream or create drama. When the other person tries to convince you by any means, repeat your decision like a broken record until they realize they are wasting their time. I have done this many times, with great success. Create your own versions. Here are take a few examples:

"Thank you for your offer, but for now, I will not accept it."

"Thank you, but I'm not interested."

"Right now, I don't want any of the products you are selling.

"I understand that you would like me to work late tonight. However, I do have prior engagements!"

"I cannot take on any more projects right now."

Repeat the same things until the other person understands you will not change your perspective or decisions. Remember that saying things by name directly and respectfully takes time and practice. And then practice again. If you have been accustomed to being silent for years, you will not become assertive overnight.

If it is difficult for you to be direct, another useful strategy is to ask for more time. You may feel nervous or not know exactly what to say. You will have time to prepare your answer and possibly use a more comfortable option, such as texting. For example: "Your request has caught me off guard. I need time to think. I'll get back to you within half an hour."

PRACTICAL SECTION

• Analyze the last conversations you had. What type of communication characterizes you most often?

• Write down some situations in which you must learn to say NO.

• Use the rehearsal behavior technique on your best friend.

5

I'M SO CONFUSED, SAD, AND LONELY. WHAT CAN I DO?

"The best and most beautiful things in the world cannot be seen or even touched. They must be felt with the heart."

— HELEN KELLER

Everything we do will certainly eventually have consequences. And, because we are accustomed to living our days by pleasing or saving those around us, there is a high probability that we will end up feeling extremely bad: depression, anxiety, deep sadness, inner emptiness, and anger. You know what I'm talking about.

Moreover, it is almost impossible not to feel overwhelmed at some point.[1] You grow weary of always helping others. You get fed up with how your desires are constantly being neglected. You even get tired of getting tired.

However, when negative emotions take control of your life, there are things you can do to regulate your emotions. And you can do this by developing positive emotions.[2]

WHY DEVELOP POSITIVE EMOTIONS?

Studies undertaken on positive emotional development show that, in the long run, this helps maximize our ability to deal with everyday life problems.[3] In other words, positive emotions lead to positive thoughts and actions. When we experience positive emotions, we become more open to new ideas, opportunities, and challenges. When we feel good, we are more likely to do what matters to us. As a result, we build physical, social, and psychological resources. Our performance is enhanced.

When you feel good, you become more creative and make better decisions. Another fascinating aspect is that positive emotions nullify the effects of negative emotions.[4] Positive emotions function as a buffer between our functioning and negative emotions.[5] **You feel good; you think better; you behave well.**

HOW TO BALANCE YOUR EMOTIONS?

There are several ways to feel more emotionally balanced, and I would like to detail as concretely as possible those that have solid scientific support:[6]

1. Cultivating joy in everyday life

Despite all the problems and difficulties we may face in life, there are many pleasures to enjoy. You may experience pleasure through your senses: smell, taste, touch, sound, and sight. In addition, there are pleasant activities that inspire joy. These activities can drive away negative emotions or make them much more bearable.

There are two major rules to follow to increase your happiness in life:

> a. Take joy in the pleasures of life.
> b. Pay attention to the positive things in your life that make you happy.

For example, if you look at a sunset, focus on what you see and the incredible sensations from that beautiful image. Be there wholly, enjoy the intense, reddish, bright shades without contaminating the sunset with other thoughts. In other words, look at the wonderful shapes and colors of the sun without responding to ten messages simultaneously. The central idea is simple. Try to be as present as you can.

How exactly do we proceed?

The first step is to make a list of activities that give us pleasure. We can add to this list anytime we find something that brings us joy. This could include enjoying a cup of tea, drinking coffee on the terrace, touching the petals of a flower and smelling the perfume, drawing, working in the garden, etc.

The second step is to choose one pleasant activity every day and do it. For example, choose to enjoy a cup of coffee in peace.

The third step is fundamental. Dedicate your body and soul to that activity, and, when you do it, do it as if it were your last. Try to remove any distractions by turning off your phone and postponing any other activities. Any activity must be carried out slowly, leisurely, giving it the necessary time and focus. Stop from time to time and become aware of the sensations you are experiencing. For example, pour the coffee into the cup slowly, listen to the sound of being poured, notice the brown color and describe it in your mind. Smell the coffee. What does it suggest to you? Feel its warmth; sip it slowly. What do you feel in your mouth? What does it remind you of? Focus on the cup in your hand, look at its color, feel its weight and appreciate the quality of the material.

If we engage in a pleasant activity, but our mind is elsewhere, the pleasure felt is diluted and minimal, and its encoding in our memory is irrelevant. But when we dedicate ourselves to it, we live it intensely, and the pleasure it gives us remains.

When you finish the activity, recall the sensations you experienced. Were they pleasant? Review them. For memories to be created, sensations must be encoded. They can be retrieved at a later stage.

Use that good mood to engage in practical activities. Exercise as often as possible and whenever appropriate to derive maximum benefit.

2. Three blessings exercise

This was introduced by Martin Seligman and is described in more detail in his book *Flourish*. It is a relatively simple technique and can be used in almost any situation. The idea behind it is to keep a daily diary. The rules mentioned above can be applied in this exercise. Force yourself to be consistent. Be present and aware. Only when you do so will you enjoy the full benefits of this exercise.

Every day, at the end of the day, write about three things, specific or general, that went well for you. For example, I watched the sunrise. I was appreciated for my work. My family is healthy and smart. Did you feel joy today? Why, what happened? Write down what things went well. Enjoy the moment. Think about the things which give your life meaning and make life worth living. I want to suggest a bold idea. Even in the darkest scenarios, there are shades of white. I studied this intervention in my dissertation on couples.

The results show that this technique is very powerful and can help reduce the symptoms of depression if sustained over a long time.[7]

For good results, try to practice this exercise every day at the same time, as much as possible. By doing so, you will develop good habits and not be able to say that you "forgot" or had other "more important" commitments. Check your schedule and find the ideal time to do so without being disturbed—for example, every night at 9 PM.

3. The secret of positive emotions

Choose a commonplace box and look at it for a few precious seconds. From now on, it will no longer be an ordinary box. I guarantee it will be different from all the boxes you have ever seen. It will be interesting, and without a doubt, it will be attractive.

Using cards, start writing down all the incredible experiences you have had, everything that has marked your life in a significant way. Put these cards into your box. As you apply this technique, you will notice that the memory of these events will bring to the surface all the wonderful emotions associated with these moments of your life. All the strong points, the joys, the achievements, the great books you have read, a special song, or the people who are important to you. Pictures, souvenirs, awards, diplomas, or favorite inspirational quotes can be included. Make sure that everything you put in the box triggers positive emotions.

When you feel depressed or overwhelmed, go straight to that special box. Look through it and remember all the good things. Use it whenever you need to understand how hard it was to get there. Don't give up; you are still a champion, even if life's troubles sometimes overwhelm you.

I hope these cognitive-behavioral strategies will help you develop positive emotions as quickly as possible. I am sure that they will do you a lot of good. You can look for other ways as well. Doing this will allow you to better communicate with others and apply everything you learned in the previous chapter about assertive communication. And you will prepare the ground for what follows in the following chapters. Keep going!

PRACTICAL SECTION

- Reflect on your activities. Note down the ones you have enjoyed the most.
- Decide how much time you will dedicate to recording the good things in your life. What time will you do this? What obstacles are you facing, and how will you overcome them?
- Take a picture of your special box. Send it to your best friend and explain its significance.

6

THE BEST WAY TO STOP YOUR CODEPENDENCY

"Thought is the blossom; language the bud; action the fruit behind it."

— RALPH WALDO EMERSON

The problem with most books and resources addressing the issue of codependency is that they are superficial. And their analysis is simple. They promise a lot but ultimately, most of the problems go unresolved. However, in the past ten years, science has allowed us to draw some accurate conclusions concerning the root cause of the problem. And I hope that this chapter will give you a much clearer perspective on the underlying mechanisms of codependency and the management of the symptoms.

People assume that emotions are caused by situations and events in their lives. So, maybe we got used to perceiving things in this way. "That suspicious person yelled at me, and I am still furious." Quite normal, isn't it? "I have an important exam tomorrow and am very anxious."

Or maybe we think in the following terms: "I have no money today and feel very anxious." The point I want to emphasize is quite simple. In each example, our minds highlight how the situation has caused our emotional response. Therefore, the first tendency is to think this way. "My parents criticized my results, and I feel so ashamed."

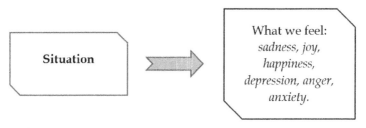

Figure 6.1.

However, according to Cognitive Behavioral Therapy, our feelings in response to a situation determine how we perceive that situation or its meaning.[1] For example, suppose ten people receive the same news: they only have a few months to live. Will they all react in the same way? Obviously not! Some will regret the risks they didn't take; some may feel guilty for the bad things they may have done. Others may feel sad, not depressed: "I lived as well as I could, and my dreams did not materialize."

Here is an interesting thing about how our mind works: our thoughts and how we interpret them trigger emotions. In other words, what we think impacts what we feel.

What happens really matters!

I don't want to say that situations alone cannot be painful. Reality matters but does not determine our reactions. When we bring thoughts into the equation, they highlight certain aspects of reality and ignore others. Some ideas will help us feel good, while others make us feel bad. The truth is that many of our thoughts are part of the inner voice that has been with us since childhood. Our beliefs come from specific experiences or the attitudes and behaviors of those who have surrounded us from an early age.

Let's take a trivial example. Let's say you hear a sound in the middle of the night. If you think "there is an intruder," you are likely to feel terror or fear and respond by running out of the room. On the other hand, if you think, "it might be my roommate disturbing the household," you will likely feel frustrated and annoyed and respond by starting an argument with them. It is simple to understand. Thus, we may have different interpretations and emotions in the same situation.

AUTOMATIC THOUGHTS

In the previous example, the event is the same: a loud sound in the middle of the night. You will think about the situation and evaluate it. In CBT, this is called *automatic thoughts*.[2] Automatic thoughts "pop" into your mind and form the particular emotion experienced (fear, guilt, annoyance, anxiety, and anger). We have a resulting behavior (escape, fighting, and avoidance).

Automatic thoughts appear in our minds without us even being aware of forming a thought in response to a particular stimulus—basically any time.

Thoughts create our feelings and emotions. Feelings influence our behavior, and behavior reinforces certain beliefs.

It is important to remember that automatic thoughts are not necessarily a statement of facts. They can be specific words, images, memories, physical sensations, or they may be based on our intuition and opinion or a sense of just knowing.

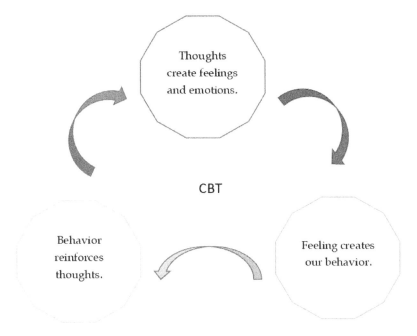

Figure 6.2.

This chapter will teach us how to challenge and change our thinking patterns. Some of our thinking patterns are so habitual that they become automatic. And just like driving, when things become automatic, we might not be conscious of them.

Our minds often distort things, especially when we have imprinted thoughts that are not in sync with our well-being. In other words, it's like a mill that is always working. The results differ depending on the expectations of that person. If you want to have a deeper perspective of the causes of mental problems, I have detailed a lot more clearly the distortions of the mind in the book, *How Does Cognitive Behavioral Therapy Work?*

THE BELIEFS WE HAVE AND CODEPENDENCY

Many things, good and bad, have been passed down to us since we were small children. Likewise, our minds have a picture of how things work. Below, I will detail some thoughts that may be most relevant to the topic discussed in this book. You will have to fight them because these thoughts are the ones that trigger and maintain codependency. Make your own list. Include the thoughts that hurt you. Unfortunately, I can't read your mind right now. It will be difficult and painful to go through this, but in the end, the results will be commensurate with the pain endured.

HOW DO WE PROCEED? ICAR PROCEDURE

I'm not going to lie to you. Changing your thinking is difficult and exhausting. That's why overcoming negative thoughts such as depression, anxiety, anger, or other problems is hard. But if we are unwilling to change the thinking patterns that cause these issues, they will always be there, and we will end up feeling worse.

The **ICAR** procedure has four fundamental stages:

- *IDENTIFICATION (I)*
- *COUNTERING (C)*
- *ALTERNATIVES (A)*
- *REPETITION (R)*

IDENTIFICATION (I)

In the first stage, the goal is to identify thoughts that bother us. You can do this by analyzing your inner language. For example, what are you telling yourself when you are depressed, anxious, or angry?

Below are some thoughts that may arise during difficult times: "I have disappointed everyone. I am a weight on others' shoulders. I'm guilty of everything that happens to me. Nobody cares about me. I'm a total failure. Nobody needs me. My needs don't matter."

Possible unhelpful thoughts:

1. I am responsible for everything around me.
2. I can never refuse those who need help.
3. What I want is not so important.
4. I'm not as special or worthy as those around me.
5. I am different from all other people.
6. Good things cannot happen to me.
7. I'm going crazy if I'm not already crazy.
8. I am not able to make my own decisions.

9. No one will ever love me.
10. Others will leave me at some point.
11. It is impossible to say no to other people's requests.
12. If I refuse to say NO, those around me will leave me.

COUNTERING (C)

Counteracting these automatic beliefs requires a change in attitude.[3] The events that led us to this point may be painful and difficult to accept. But we must deal with whatever happened to us. By counteracting bad thoughts, those thoughts will lose their power. For someone drained by negative thinking, this countering process is one of the most difficult things to do. However, we have to try. Below I will share with you several ways we can deal with negative thoughts:

1. Counteracting at the behavioral level

This can be done by creating new behavioral patterns through experimentation or by doing the exact opposite of what negative thoughts tell you to do.

Counteracting through behavioral experimentation involves creating experiences through which you can directly test the thoughts that upset you. It is one of the most effective methods because the mind learns better this way. This technique involves choosing a thought and creating a situation through which we can directly test it to check its veracity. For example, suppose one of the thoughts you strongly believe in is, "If I refuse to say NO, those around me will leave me alone."

How do we proceed? We can approach our friends and ask them if they would really leave us. You will be surprised to realize how much your thoughts can differ from reality. Behavioral experiments are based on the thoughts you have identified. Find creative and suitable variations through which you can test the validity of your thoughts or what your mind invents.

Counteracting by technique: Do the exact opposite of what your mind tells you

This is a useful strategy because it shows us we can initiate an action contrary to the thought we have in mind. For example, if your thoughts tell you to flee into the desert and isolate yourself from everyone, do the exact opposite; deliberately seek contact with others. If the thought tells you that nothing makes sense, do something meaningful and valuable that makes sense. You can use both behavioral experiment strategies or do the exact opposite of what your mind tells you, depending on the type of thoughts that upset you.

2. Counteracting at the mind level

It is one of psychotherapy's most used tools for disputing thoughts. The most common techniques for restructuring our thoughts are evidence analysis, logical analysis, pragmatic analysis, metaphors, and narratives.[4]

Evidence analysis

Suppose the thought that stops you from doing something to feel better is, "Nothing makes me feel better." Our task is to see if this thought is supported by evidence. Simply put, question this idea. Was there anything today or yesterday that made you feel better? Generally, you will be surprised to find that there were such things.

Whether it's a cup of tea you drank, a walk, or a conversation, use the questions to analyze the thought: Is there nothing I can do to make myself feel a little better? This way, you will notice how that negative thought begins to lose their power.

Remember. You are like a great lawyer, asking questions that challenge your thoughts, beliefs, and expectations, ultimately testing and challenging whether or not they stand true and whether they help or hinder you.

It involves challenging the general conclusions you have drawn from a particular event. For example, it is possible you were wrong when you concluded: "Life is a burden. She forgot about me. Nobody cares about me." You came to such a conclusion because you applied a general rule to a specific situation.

Use questions to examine thoughts and correct erroneous conclusions. For instance:

- Has life always been a burden?
- Is it logical to think it is a burden just because I am going through a difficult situation right now?
- Can I interpret this thought differently?
- How might someone else view the situation?

Pragmatic analysis

This is one of the strategies that patients prefer. It involves examining the usefulness of a thought. For example, suppose that the negative thought goes like this: "I'm usually not good at anything; it makes no sense to try anything else."

The next step is to examine the impact this thought has on you. Does thinking like this help you? How do you feel when you assume you are nobody and nothing you do is relevant? When this thought comes to mind, which actions do you follow?

ALTERNATIVES (A)

It is not enough to eliminate those negative thoughts that keep us depressed, anxious, guilty, or codependent; it is necessary to replace them with positive ones.

Another mental, healthy, and undistorted content is a functional alternative. For example, if you believed for a long time that "Nothing makes me happy," a healthy alternative to this belief may be: "There is still one thing or a few things I can do that bring me joy." It may be drinking a cup of tea or going for a walk with friends.

When you notice the negative thought popping into your mind again, remember it is false and remind yourself of the actual and functional version. Then, repeat this functional variant until you see that the negative thought has gone and no longer represents a danger to you.

REPETITIONS (R)

Even if it's not true, most of the patients I worked with believe that the problem has been solved if they won the battle with a specific thought at some point. But this is a misconception. If you have reinforced a false belief by repeating it 1,000 times, you won't solve the problem by repeating the functional version only 100 times. It takes repetition and patience.

The truth will set you free, but it must be repeated every time the lie reappears. If you tell yourself 1,000 times that you are a loser who didn't achieve anything and ten times that some things you did were good— what do you think will have more impact upon you: those 1,000 negative thoughts or those few positive statements? The key is to repeat the entire process until you reach the point where you are fully convinced that you have won the battle with that specific thought. Negative thoughts may happen in different situations. Repeat the process until you see that the truth has set you free.

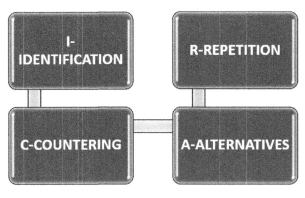

Figure 6.3.

Don't give up

I want to share this great quote: "Bad thinking is any uncontrolled thought. Thoughts must serve us, not tyrannize us," Richard Wurmbrand.

You may not be able to counteract certain thoughts. And this is normal. But don't give up. Negative thoughts lead to destructive emotions.

At the end of this chapter, I want to remind you that a healthy thinking life leads to a healthy mind. Negative thoughts cause and sustain depression, anxiety, anger, and codependency. It is important to remember that our thinking is the most vulnerable area of the mind.

With some help from the strategies mentioned in the previous chapter, it will be easier for you to change specific thoughts. Emotions often also influence thoughts, even if thoughts are the ones that create the emotions. So, hang in there. I hope you will have the clarity to identify destructive thoughts, counteract them, and consistently replace them with healthy, true, positive ones.

PRACTICAL SECTION

- What are your most common thoughts that cause and sustain your addiction? Write them down carefully.
- Plan a behavioral experiment this week by choosing one of your negative thoughts. Write down what you expect to happen at the beginning and, then at the end, what actually happened. What are the differences? What did you learn?
- What are the four steps of the ICAR strategy?
- Make cards on which you write the alternative version of your destructive thoughts. Write down how you feel when you win the battle with one thought: happy, strong, confident, ambitious, hopeful.

7

START TO GAIN AUTONOMY

"Autonomy is different from independence. It means acting with choice."

— DANIEL H. PINK

If you are fighting a fierce battle with codependency, one of the most common questions that maintain it is: What do you think I should do?

Codependency is characterized by an inability to attain true autonomy and independence. You are afraid of making your own decisions. You are scared to have your own plans and ideas. You're afraid to know what you want. You freeze at the idea that decisions can be entirely yours. The thought that you may have your own values and abilities to fulfill your dreams may seem overwhelming because your mind was conditioned to live for someone else. Maybe you are paralyzed at the thought of making even the smallest decisions. And when you do so, it can be terrifying. But fundamental to healing from codependency is autonomy. And this chapter is an extra step in this journey.

WHY DO YOU NEED TO DEVELOP AUTONOMY?

Autonomy also means freedom. And it is that freedom that brings confidence. Your self-esteem increases as your independence grows. If you are an autonomous person, you trust your own decisions and initiatives. You take control and make plans. You operate independently. You make informed, conscious, deliberate decisions without involving other people. In other words, you operate on your terms.[1] And you enjoy yourself and everything. And, gradually, fear and insecurity are replaced by trust because you know you have the skills to deal with the problems in your world.

I'm not trying to deceive you; having autonomy is hard, but it's wonderful. There are many reasons why it's worth persevering. I will mention only a few of them. First of all, autonomous people are happier and more involved in what they do. They feel valuable and motivated to keep developing new skills.[2] They create things. They always try and usually keep their heads high in all the battles—whether won or lost. Of course, they probably fail more than most people.

But they probably learn a lot more too. They live life exactly on the terms they consider relevant. They are real titans, and that's exactly what I want you to become. In fact, **AUTONOMY IS EXACTLY THE OPPOSITE OF CODEPENDENCY**. It's precisely where we want to end up.

STEPS THAT OPEN THE ROAD TO AUTONOMY

1. Start redefining your mindset

There are many reasons we may have lost our confidence in thinking clearly and making things work. When we believe in lies and lie to ourselves (self-denial), in chaos and distrust of what we can do, our ability to think appropriately deteriorates. And gradually, we become more confused and insecure.

Slowly we start to hate ourselves and repeat that we only make stupid decisions. We worry and deny our needs and become tired, overwhelmed, depressed, and anxious.

But I want to emphasize something. You can change your mindset. Your mind can function on other levels. You can figure things out. You can make decisions. You can figure out what your needs and values are. You can also work on improving your self-esteem. You can be rational. You can evaluate your behavior and become a better version of yourself.

All of these things are possible if you start working on changing your beliefs. Using the ICAR strategy described in the previous chapter, you will gradually tear down your old ideas and build a new foundation. Then, you will be able to change the outcomes. And, small victories you achieve will help you create a new mindset. So use this strategy; do not ignore it. It is one of the best ways to understand that YOU CAN!

2. Establish your core values and why your life has value

If you have lived your life thinking, planning, speaking, imagining, and deciding what others want, it will be difficult to determine your own values and why your life has value. If your passions, dreams, and goals are unclear, you will be like a ship with no rudder. But there are two big problems: it doesn't know where it is heading and can't change direction because it doesn't have a compass. So, if you bought this book and read these lines, it means that the time has come for you to realize what direction you are heading in and to go on the offensive. All great warriors know how to choose their battles. And so, you will face a new battle.

I want to respect you. And this respect involves telling you the truth. Discovering your values and why life has value is not a one-page job. Nor is it a one-day job, nor even a chapter. It's hard work and exhausting; it may take months or years.

Most of the books that address this topic talk about the fact that you should pursue your passions, dreams, and goals, but very few tell you exactly how to do that. The next chapter will therefore be dedicated in its entirety to this subject. And I believe your chances to earn autonomy will improve radically. But changes will be slow and energy-consuming. However, the result will give you the strength and courage to fight the fight.

3. Take full responsibility

Remember that no one will come after you to save you. Did you hear me right? **NO ONE WILL COME TO SAVE YOU!** Not your best friend, not your parents, not your wife, probably not God himself! And I believe in God. You will never develop confidence if you rely on others to meet your needs. If you let others perform life's tasks for you, you will become discouraged.

The first step is to notice those situations in which you depend on those around you. Then, gradually start doing simple things on your own. Then raise the stakes and do more. If an opportunity comes up that would suit you, evaluate it from all angles. You are the only one who can change the situation you are in at present. A famous French philosopher, Sartre, used to say that it doesn't matter what life made of us. It matters what we do with what's left.

Another equally important step is to apply all the strategies and tools I give you in this book. Then, work on the practical sections. By doing so, you will have achieved some crucial victories. Finally, where necessary, look for alternative resources to help you succeed.

PRACTICAL SECTION

- What is the opposite of codependency for you?
- Write down some specific situations that required taking responsibility.
- Build a list of thoughts that need to be removed from your mindset using the ICAR strategy.
- Reward yourself for all the work done so far; maybe a pizza?

8

THE SECRET OF DETACHMENT

"The meaning of Life is to find your gift. The purpose of Life is to give it away."

— PABLO PICASSO

One day, I was with a patient who made a disturbing statement:" *I missed my life. I'm 67 years old and haven't lived one moment of my life for myself. What the hell am I supposed to do with that?"*

He was a remarkable man who had had tremendous success. He solved everyone's problems. And why not? He was the C.E.O, after all. He always took care of everything, but he felt the world lay on his shoulders. He always put others' needs above his own. I want you to reflect on an important aspect. Now is the time to stop caring for everyone else and examine your needs.

IT'S NOT ABOUT SELFISHNESS

As you can see, I'm a supporter of sharing. I like to give to those around me, and I think this is a critical aspect of being human: having nobler and higher goals in life. But at the same time, it is also essential to understand that we can only give to those around us when we know what we have to give. What can we offer them? What are the best values we can pass on? How do we work best to help the next person? I hope we do not reach the age of 67 and conclude that we have completely missed the mark. And that's why I'm writing these lines.

In all the noise of everyday life, many things have to be done daily, and most of us do them subconsciously. We simply do them. No feedback, no reflection. And because so many of these tasks are repetitive, we forget what really matters.

I would like you to answer a few questions that may trouble you. What do you live for? What are your values? Did you live your life, or did you live according to a script written by others, for instance, parents, boyfriend, employer, or teacher?

When we live our lives how others say we should, we gradually develop anxiety, depression, and other problems such as codependency traits. Therefore, it becomes necessary to identify our values. We can find our purpose in life by determining what is of value to us. Conversely, if you live according to other people's values, you are defined as codependent.

HOW CAN WE DISCOVER OUR OWN VALUES?

- Determine things that are really important and write them down

Take an A4 sheet, divide it into four equal parts, and then again into another four. Next, take eight or ten cards. Note on each card something important to you: health, money, success, career, children, and friendships. Don't rush, sit, reflect, and think. Place the cards on a table before you. Next, we will use a strategy called "forced choice."

You should put one of the cards aside every minute and a half. It's like giving up that value: I can live without money. I can live without eroticism. After another minute and a half, put aside something else. After a minute and a half, take out another value. Put the card aside, even if you oppose it.

That way, you'll end up with one on the table. The one you kept last has a rank of 1. Give all the other cards a number in the exact order you took them out. So, you have built a ranking by eliminating specific options.

Once you have this ranking, write them down in a column. Look at a regular day in your life and write down all the activities performed every hour. Create enough templates to cover several days. In one column, you have your values, and in another, the actions you undertake on a regular day. List your activities that day and match them to your most important values.

Then go on to the next value. For the second value, look at the activities you perform. By doing this, we try to see if there is any congruence between what we think is important and what we actually do. It is necessary to see where we allocate our resources. If what we value harms us, it is not worth our time. For example, if professionalism comes first, what percentage of the day did I spend on professionalism? Use examples to highlight what professionalism means. For example, professionalism may mean working ten hours a day while being as focused as possible. Is friendship important? Okay, how much of our time have we allocated to friendship?

The inconsistency or incompatibility between values and how we live may lead to illness. We should reflect on this relationship. What is really important to me? How do I think about my mind, time, and emotions? We often postpone reflecting on values and our time. What is really important? If the health of my mind is essential, how many resources am I willing to allocate to it? This process is often painful and unpleasant. But it brings with it the chance to change what needs to be changed. It is vital to do this exercise from time to time. We are then less likely not to live life according to a script written by those around us.

THE MOST RELEVANT QUESTIONS OF LIFE

The following concepts were presented at one of the courses I attended. They impressed me greatly. The wonderful teacher asked us three questions that have stayed with me ever since. These questions are still in my mind today. And I would like to present them to you exactly as they were asked. They did not give me peace until I had thoroughly evaluated my life. But in the end, they helped me a lot. If you repeat these questions constantly, there is a good chance that you will not reach the age of 67 and realize that life has passed you. As Nietzsche used to say, live life at its time, so you will be proud of yourself and help those around you.

1. **What exactly do you live for?**
2. **What exactly would you be willing to die for?**
3. **Did you live the way you wanted to?**

At some point, things can no longer be changed. It is, therefore, crucial to find the answers to these questions early on. Use this strategy as a compass to move forward and get exactly where you want to be. Whatever it is, we can't fool our minds. Instead, we can live a meaningful life. We are happier and have more confidence in ourselves when we live according to what we think is important.

PRACTICAL SECTION

- Name three of your most important values.
- Analyze the congruence between the values you have and your actions. What do they prove?
- Write a letter to yourself to answer the three questions at the end of this chapter.

9

THE COURAGE TO CHANGE: START TO PAINT YOUR GOALS

"Do not wait; the time will never be just right. Start where you stand, and work with whatever tools you may have at your command, and better tools will be found as you go along."

— GEORGE HERBERT

In conversation with a college classmate, she asked me if I always knew exactly what I wanted to do or if I did things in the hope that, in time, I would discover what I wanted to do. I tried to answer her as honestly as possible: Who knows exactly what he wants to do? There is a lot of chaos in the world. But as you start to put things together, you will get a clear picture of what suits you and what you want to do. Therefore, if you have indications where your values lie, follow them.

Later, other clues will emerge, and then others. Do you have any clues? They are like archaeological excavations. Go back to the previous chapter and work toward understanding your values. If you fail, look for a good therapist to guide you.

THE COURAGE TO HAVE CLEAR GOALS

We are not codependent. We are human beings who have developed certain codependent traits. And I want you to keep this in mind. I will return to this subject in the next chapter. But until then, I want to point out that these codependent traits often don't allow us to enjoy the luxury of setting clear goals because we don't analyze what we want or where we are heading. We always carry the burden of caring for others. We do not consider that we deserve to have good things happening to us.

Goals give us clear directions and meaning. They can be daily, weekly, monthly, or annual. I encourage you to have one from each category. For example, suppose you want to get to Rome. If you get on the first plane you find and hope to get there, it probably won't happen. Making this a goal means planning and going directly to your location. In other words, don't just do things by chance and hope you will eventually get where you want. So it is with life. It is worth living with a higher level of awareness. Work towards a goal every day. You don't have to have all the data in place at the beginning, but it's important to start with a plan.

Goals can also be quite fun. They often generate enthusiasm and motivation. Do you get bored? Antidote: Start setting goals.[1] When you set a specific goal, you will feel physically stronger, more energetic, and more enthusiastic. You are motivated because you have a pretty good idea of what you want. You embark on a course where your whole being, including the subconscious mind, works to achieve that goal. We can't fool our minds. If our subconscious mind is not engaged in achieving a goal, we might hesitate; we will feel confused and paralyzed. If the conscious and subconscious minds are involved, we will gradually begin to do things automatically.[2]

HOW TO APPROACH THINGS

1. From a desire to a goal

We often want good things. Therefore, the problem does not appear at the level of desire. We want to be healthier, free, strong, and autonomous. And this is the first step. It is highly relevant but ultimately not enough. The RUBICON model[3] addresses this issue in more detail. When we have a wish, it must be defined in behavioral terms. For example, I want to work on codependency traits: I must therefore keep a journal of my emotions, record my needs, and fight negative thoughts using the ICAR procedure. Once you understand your wants, associate them with clear behaviors. By doing so, you will break your wants into manageable pieces.

2. Check the congruence between objectives and behavior periodically

Suppose your goal is to be as autonomous as possible and reduce the codependent traits. What have you done today to align your behavior to your intentions? What did you do last week? What did you do last month? You can hold yourself accountable for your behavior by asking this type of question. Maybe you set out to read a book that details the symptoms more clearly or conveys certain things to your partner. You get the idea. You can even start giving yourself a grade every day. How much attention did I pay to my goal? Give yourself a score from 1 to 10. This way, it is possible to note if you are living life according to your goals and objectives. And there is a vast difference between living in congruence with purpose and just wanting to live that way. So the question is: How will I know that I am working on my goal and have managed to achieve it?[4]

3. Write down your goals

Maybe your goal is to break this codependency bond in your relationship. Or stop waiting for validation, approval, and partner's attention; be more careful with your thoughts, emotions, and desires; and feel good even when your partner is not there for you.

Write down this goal as clearly as possible and place it where so you can see it. Use the closet, desk, or phone background. Any place you go to or visit often. As we write what we want, the subconscious mind gradually comes to understand this as well. And the chances of success are much higher. Our attention and concentration work much better when we note what tasks we must perform.

4. Reward yourself for your work

The tendency is to reward ourselves at the end of a battle. In that case, the reward is too far away, and we lose patience. If, by the end of the day, you decide that you have worked to achieve your goals, give yourself a quick reward. Our mind has a habit of repeating the actions it considers pleasant and avoiding those that are painful.[5] This is simply how we are conditioned. So, take that short walk, reward yourself with a good cup of tea, and pamper yourself when you manage to keep up. Gradually, your mind will associate that action with the positive emotions you get from the rewards. If you want to take things to the next level, penalize behaviors that do not conform to your values and goals—for example, saying, Yes, when you want to say NO. If you punish those behaviors appropriately, your mind will learn to associate them with discomfort and start to avoid them.[6]

PRACTICAL SECTION

- Formulate general long- and short-term goals: to communicate more clearly, to visit Rome, to go on holiday alone, to practice a hobby, etc.
- For each goal, establish the corresponding action: for example, if you want to communicate better: read aloud for twenty minutes; if you want to be more assertive with a friend, write down what you feel, think, or want.
- Analyze to what extent your ultimate goal and your actions correspond. On a scale of 1 to 10, how much do you think your actions will help you reach the goal?
- Think about a goal that you achieved: whether it was a daily, weekly, monthly, or annual goal. What reward did you give yourself for reaching it?

10

SMART SIMPLE PRINCIPLES TO BEAT CODEPENDENCY

"I hated every minute of training, but I said: Don't quit. Suffer now and live the rest of your life as a champion."

— MUHAMMAD ALI

I intend to be as short and specific as possible with this book. I have almost reached the end of the journey, and I feel happy that I am leaving the reader with much more information than when we started. I do not claim to have fully understood how codependency works, but I have a much clearer idea of what can be done. I therefore want to leave you with some clear principles to help you win this battle.

I hope these will be strong pillars to lean on when things go crazy. At the same time, I hope they will light your way, just as a simple candle often lights darkness. I read a beautiful piece of writing and want to share it with you: *"There is no denying the fact that there is evil in this world, but the light will always conquer the darkness."*

FIRST PRINCIPLE: DO EXACTLY WHAT YOU SAY YOU'RE GOING TO DO

You will not become victorious when you doubt yourself and don't know exactly who you are. One of the best ways to build your self-esteem is to keep your word. This is crucial. For instance, if you have said that you will apply the strategies described here, don't hesitate. Do so. If you say you will be assertive tonight, do so, no matter what. If you say you will turn down a friend because you have different plans, then do so.

This is how you build confidence. If you keep your promises, your mind will know you are serious, and you will trust yourself. You will create a reputation for yourself over time. You don't need external sources of approval. Keep the promises you make. If you promise to wake up at 6 a.m. to go to training, do it. You promised. Take yourself seriously.

SECOND PRINCIPLE: GUARD YOUR BELIEFS CAREFULLY

It is essential to pay attention to how we think. Many of our beliefs have been developed over a lifetime. We already know how problems are formed and maintained. You were not born with doubt; you were not born depressed and discouraged or thinking that you are worthless. All these beliefs have been placed on you by external sources. These may be overprotective parents or parents who have not given you the attention and support you need. These could even be teachers, friends, or people we don't remember.

It's simple: if you think like a person with codependent traits, that's how you'll define yourself and behave in the long term. If you feel that you are not important and what you think is not relevant, I assure you that you will find evidence to confirm this. If you do not find proof, you will constantly manufacture proof. So use the ICAR procedures often and look for other ways to focus on your thoughts and beliefs. Derive your emotions and behaviors from them. A destructive thought is bad as long as it hurts you.

One of the most common schemes or patterns you may face is subjugation.[1] It manifests in constantly letting others control or dominate your behavior or emotions. This comes from a fear of being abandoned, unloved, or seen as selfish. Therefore, this is one of the most critical issues that we need to keep in mind.

THIRD PRINCIPLE: YOU ARE NOT CODEPENDENT; YOU ARE A HUMAN BEING

The chances are that next year you will find yourself in the same position as you are now. Codependent patterns can be difficult to break for two reasons: you are not working through your problems and are not making the required changes. For the results to be lasting, it is necessary to work on changing your own identity. This involves changing your perspective on the world and yourself, including your preconceptions about yourself.

Think of two people working to leave behind codependent traits. The first is tempted to enter into a dysfunctional relationship but realizes in time and says: "no, I try not to be a codependent." The other says, "I don't want that; I'm not codependent." There is a slight difference here, but the latter shows a change in self-belief. You have identified your true self. This includes getting to know yourself—what you enjoy, what is important to you, and your goals and needs. As a result, you no longer define yourself as codependent. However, it is difficult to change your identity if you do not change your belief in yourself.

The more fulfilled you are with one aspect of your identity, the more motivated you are to maintain the associated behaviors and actions. For example, if you are proud of your autonomy, you will be happy to spend time alone; stop feeling guilt, and express your emotions. Learn to communicate, and you will do it more and more often. It's simple; codependent traits reflect your identity and beliefs. Therefore, be careful of the words you use to describe yourself. Guard and reflect on the thoughts that live in your mind: how to change your identity? Review the strategies and tools that a free, autonomous, independent person follows. You already have some of the necessary tools I described in this book. When you have the opportunity, decide what kind of person you want to be. And do it precisely because you are not codependent. You are a free and human person who wants to change some of your traits.

FOURTH PRINCIPLE: TAKE CARE OF YOUR RELATIONSHIP

Let me ask you a humble question: Why do you think you still have codependent traits? Think about it. These traits were planted and watered in your relationships. You probably chose relationships that match your codependent behaviors.

You probably chose a partner who encourages codependency. Why? Because it's a way of life you understand. It would be uncomfortable to be with someone who does not fit the pattern and your way of thinking. For example, if you are convinced that you are inadequate, you will choose a partner who will make you feel inferior—because that's how you really think about yourself. You will funnel your energy into supporting your partner without considering what you need for yourself. It's easy for you to be like that—it's part of your belief system. So pay attention to beliefs and how they are sustained.

So evaluate your relationships. Analyze them. If you want to keep in touch, do so. But tell your partner or your friends honestly what you know now and how you would like things to be in the future. Use the assertive communication we discussed earlier. However, if you have done nothing to address the codependency, it will not simply go away. You need the support and understanding of those close to you. Otherwise, you may want to reevaluate your options a bit.

FIFTH PRINCIPLE: CONTROL ONLY WHAT YOU CAN CONTROL

There are three ways we can respond to codependency.[2] The first is surrender. You feel helpless and give up without a fight. You consider yourself an unhappy victim without the power to change anything. The second is avoidance. In simple terms, this is when you act as if nothing has happened. You don't care anymore. All you do is protect yourself as much as possible from any potential danger. The third type of response is overcompensation. This happens when those around you say that your only desire is to control everything. Because you feel subjugated, you accuse, cry, beg, blame, and threaten to hurt yourself. That's where that intense rage originates from.

AMAZING MINDFULNESS EXERCISE

There are many things we can control. Like much of our recovery. But we will be unable to control what others do or how others respond to our healing. So we must accept what we cannot control. Things are as they are. And acceptance is, of course, a skill and an art that can be learned. Mindfulness is one of the best strategies for learning to look at and accept things as they are without judging or evaluating them.[3] Therefore, I want to end this book by giving you a mindfulness exercise you can practice whenever you think you need to disconnect.

This exercise aims to help you disconnect from stressful thoughts, scenarios, and emotions and focus on what is happening in the present. It is important to point out that we often live in the past or the future. We do not enjoy what we have now. We do not notice the small changes that are happening now.

How do we proceed?

Choose a candle and position it in front of you at a distance of 20 to 30 centimeters. It can be plain or fragrant. Inhale and exhale deeply. Inhale for four seconds, hold your breath for one second, and then exhale for four seconds. Watch the flame of this candle for three minutes. Do it calmly and in a detached manner. Relax, don't frown. You will notice that different changes will take place inside the candle. Observe them all with detachment. Thoughts will pop into your mind. Inhale for four seconds, hold the air for a second and exhale for four seconds. Come back to the candle. What do you see? How is its flame? What colors can you identify? You will notice how wax accumulates around the base of the candle.

Observe but do not judge. This means not getting carried away with the thoughts. They are there, you see them, but you ignore them. Let your thoughts pass like the clouds pass through the sky. At some point, the mind will calm down, and the thoughts will calm down. You will feel some peace. Enjoy this special moment. Practice this twice daily for at least a few weeks to enhance its effectiveness.[4] Repetition is the key. I hope this technique will be helpful. I sometimes use it to relax and suggest it to patients who need it. Take care of your mind and heart!

CONCLUSION

I have written this short book for people who need to find practical solutions to their problems. Although plenty of books address this issue, I was not satisfied with their proposed solutions. Many of them seemed very superficial and difficult to apply in our day-to-day life. I therefore decided to focus my writing on just some of the specific problems reported by those with codependent traits. And I want to be honest; it wasn't easy at all.

This book is not just an opinion. Here you won't find my beliefs and my ideas. I studied hard and tried to review the literature to find evidence-based information. Then I wrote this book based on my short experience in clinical practice. I'm still in the early stages. So, be patient with me and then with yourself. I hope this book is informative and can provide you with all the tools you need to achieve your goals.

CONCLUSION

We have reached the end of this journey, and this is a good and encouraging sign. I want to congratulate all of you who have shown interest and patience and come this far, investing in the most beautiful thing: your mind. The next step is to implement what you have learned in real life. Be consistent, and you will be rewarded. Your problems have probably developed over time. The recovery will therefore take some time too.

Because I am always looking to improve, I will greatly appreciate your honest feedback. I want to make things better in the future, so you can share your opinion by leaving an honest review on Amazon. Here are the link and QR code where you can do so: https://www.amazon.com/review/create-review/?asin=B08VC839C5.

I wish you good health and take care of yourself.

P.S. If you are fighting similar problems and want me to write about them, please let me know what they are, and I will do my best to write about them.

DO YOU FEEL INCOMPLETE WITHOUT YOUR PARTNER?

Are you engaging in toxic behavior because you don't want to be alone?

Then…. you may also like

Codepenent No More: From Being Needy & Clingy to Having Amazing, Authentic, and Loving Relationships

This book is the 2nd one in the *"Codependent No More Series."* The author focuses more on what to do after getting rid of those codependent traits and how to build amazing, authentic & loving relationships.

Here is a fraction of what you'll discover:

- **Practical exercises** to help you assess your relationships and take steps to transform your life
- The 7 red flags that indicate you've fallen into a codependent relationship

- Answers to the most frequently asked questions people have about their dynamics with others
- How to help someone who is codependent without making them defensive or ruining your relationship
- **What *not* to do when you find yourself free from a codependent relationship**
- Resources and tools to encourage your emotional development and build a support system
- What attachment styles are and how they are affecting your relationship without you even realizing it
- **The secret to setting healthy boundaries** and why they're so important for reclaiming your time and energy
- How to develop effective communication strategies and solve codependency conflicts

And much more.

Scan the QR code now to discover what it takes to have a healthy and loving relationship.

NOTES

1. CODEPENDENCY: HOW DO I RECOGNIZE IT?

1. Bacon, I., McKay, E., Reynolds, F., & McIntyre, A. (2020). The lived experience of codependency: An interpretative phenomenological analysis. International Journal of Mental Health and Addiction, 18(3), 754-771.
2. Morgan Jr, J. P. (1991). What is codependency?. Journal of clinical psychology, 47(5), 720-729.
3. Martsolf, D. S., Sedlak, C. A., & Doheny, M. O. (2000). Codependency and related health variables. Archives of psychiatric nursing, 14(3), 150-158.
4. Reyome, N. D., & Ward, K. S. (2007). Self-reported history of childhood maltreatment and codependency in undergraduate nursing students. Journal of Emotional Abuse, 7(1), 37-50.
5. Johnston, C., Dorahy, M. J., Courtney, D., Bayles, T., & O'Kane, M. (2009). Dysfunctional schema modes, childhood trauma and dissociation in borderline personality disorder. Journal of behavior therapy and experimental psychiatry, 40(2), 248-255.

2. WHAT DO CODEPENDENT RELATIONSHIPS LOOK LIKE?

1. Cermak, T. L. (1986). Diagnostic criteria for codependency. Journal of psychoactive drugs, 18(1), 15-20.
2. Friel, J.C. (1985). Codependency assessment inventory: A preliminary research tool. Focus on the Family and Chemical Dependency, 8(1), 20-21.

3. I'M CODEPENDENT, NOW WHAT?

1. Cramer, P. (2000). Defense mechanisms in psychology today: Further processes for adaptation. American Psychologist, 55(6), 637.

4. HOW TO STOP BEING A PEOPLE-PLEASER

1. Easterlin, R. A. (2003). Explaining happiness. Proceedings of the National Academy of Sciences, 100(19), 11176-11183.
2. UK Violence Intervention and Prevention Center. The Four Basic Styles of Communication.
3. Antony, M. The Shyness and Social Anxiety Workbook, 2010.
4. Rancer, A. S., & Avtgis, T. A. (2006). Argumentative and aggressive communication: Theory, research, and application. Sage.
5. Pipas, M. D., & Jaradat, M. (2010). Assertive communication skills. Annales Universitatis Apulensis: Series Oeconomica, 12(2), 649.

5. I'M SO CONFUSED, SAD, AND LONELY. WHAT CAN I DO?

1. Anderson, N. T., & Miller, R. (2002). Getting anger under control: Overcoming unresolved resentment, overwhelming emotions, and the lies behind anger. Harvest House Publishers.
2. Carl, J. R., Soskin, D. P., Kerns, C., & Barlow, D. H. (2013). Positive emotion regulation in emotional disorders: A theoretical review. Clinical psychology review, 33(3), 343-360.
3. Fredrickson, B. L., Mancuso, R. A., Branigan, C., & Tugade, M. M. (2000). The undoing effect of positive emotions. Motivation and emotion, 24(4), 237-258.
4. Fredrickson, B. L. (2004). The broaden–and–build theory of positive emotions. Philosophical Transactions of the Royal Society of London. Series B: Biological Sciences, 359(1449), 1367-1377.
5. Fredrickson, B. L., & Branigan, C. (2005). Positive emotions broaden the scope of attention and thought-action repertoires. Cognition & emotion,

19(3), 313-332.
6. Quoidbach, J., Mikolajczak, M., & Gross, J. J. (2015). Positive interventions: An emotion regulation perspective. Psychological bulletin, 141(3), 655.
7. Watkins, P. C., Woodward, K., Stone, T., & Kolts, R. L. (2003). Gratitude and happiness: Development of a measure of gratitude, and relationships with subjective well-being. Social Behavior and Personality: an international journal, 31(5), 431-451.

6. THE BEST WAY TO STOP YOUR CODEPENDENCY

1. Howes, J. L., & Parrott, C. A. (1991). Conceptualization and flexibility in cognitive therapy. In The Challenge of Cognitive Therapy (pp. 25-42). Springer, Boston, MA.
2.
3. https://www.therapistaid.com/therapy-guide/cognitive-restructuring
4. Young, J. E., Rygh, J. L., Weinberger, A. D., & Beck, A. T. (2014). Cognitive therapy for depression.

7. START TO GAIN AUTONOMY

1. Deci, E. L., & Ryan, R. M. (1995). Human autonomy. In Efficacy, agency, and self-esteem (pp. 31-49). Springer, Boston, MA.
2. Lin, B. Y. J., Lin, Y. K., Lin, C. C., & Lin, T. T. (2013). Job autonomy, its predispositions and its relation to work outcomes in community health centers in Taiwan. Health Promotion International, 28(2), 166-177.

9. THE COURAGE TO CHANGE: START TO PAINT YOUR GOALS

1. Rusk, N., Tamir, M., & Rothbaum, F. (2011). Performance and learning goals for emotion regulation. Motivation and Emotion, 35(4), 444-460.
2. Thinking fast and slow- Daniel Kahneman.

3. Spiess, E., & Wittmann, A. (1999). Motivational phases associated with the foreign placement of managerial candidates: an application of the Rubicon model of action phases. International Journal of Human Resource Management, 10(5), 891-905.
4. Graham, S., & Hebert, M. (2011). Writing to read: A meta-analysis of the impact of writing and writing instruction on reading. Harvard Educational Review, 81(4), 710-744.
5. Atomic Habits James Clear.
6. McLeod, S. (2015). Skinner-operant conditioning. Retrieved from.

10. SMART SIMPLE PRINCIPLES TO BEAT CODEPENDENCY

1. Young, J. E., Klosko, J. S., & Weishaar, M. E. (2003). Schema therapy. New York: Guilford, 254.
2. Young, J. E., Klosko, J. S., & Weishaar, M. E. (2006). Schema therapy: A practitioner's guide. Guilford Press.
3. Chiesa, A., & Serretti, A. (2009). Mindfulness-based stress reduction for stress management in healthy people: a review and meta-analysis. The journal of alternative and complementary medicine, 15(5), 593-600.
4. Baer, R. A. (2003). Mindfulness training as a clinical intervention: A conceptual and empirical review. Clinical psychology: Science and practice, 10(2), 125-143.

BIBLIOGRAPHY

Made in the USA
Las Vegas, NV
20 September 2022